P.S. I want to thank Ash Carter and Yolanda Cuomo for making this little book possible.

Jean Pigozzi

ME + CO

The Selfies: 1972–2017

BOOK DESIGN BY YOLANDA CUOMO, NYC

Associate Designer: Bonnie Briant

Assistant Designer: Bobbie Richardson

Assistant to Jean Pigozzi: Yoni Markman

Reproduction and Print Preparation: John Weisenberger

Published by Damiani

info@damianieditore.com

www.damianieditore.com

Printed in May 2017 by Grafiche Damiani—Faenza Group SpA, Italy.

ISBN 978-88-6208-550-2

All author proceeds from the sale of this book will support (RED)'s fight against AIDS.

(RED)®

(RED) was created by Bono and Bobby Shriver in 2006 to transform the collective power of consumers into a global force of critical, life-saving funding for the AIDS fight. (RED) works with the world's most iconic brands to develop (RED)-branded products and experiences that, when purchased, trigger corporate contributions to the Global Fund.

To date, (RED) has generated $465 million for the Global Fund to fight AIDS, Tuberculosis, and Malaria. 100 percent of that money goes to work on the ground, supporting HIV/AIDS grants in Ghana, Kenya, Lesotho, Rwanda, South Africa, Swaziland, Tanzania, and Zambia. Global Fund (RED) grants have impacted more than 90 million people through prevention, treatment, counseling, HIV testing, and care services.

(RED) is a division of The ONE Campaign. Learn more at www.red.org.

"Despite Western society's broad access to economical domestic cameras capable of capturing self-portraits . . . the selfie did not emerge" until very recently, academic Karen Ann Donnachie writes in "Selfies, #me: Glimpses of Authenticity in the Narcissus' Pool of the Networked Amateur Self-Portrait," among the first, and one hopes the last, scholarly deconstructions of the subject. "Our own cultural memory corroborates the theory that it just wasn't something that you did."

"When digital cameras came out, it made it much easier because you could miss," Pigozzi says. "You can take a hundred pictures and then erase the memory. It's one of the few things that are completely free in life. With iPhones, you can see yourself taking a selfie, so you can get it right." In the nineteenth century, Oliver Wendell Holmes, Sr. called the daguerrotype "a mirror with a memory." With a front-facing cell phone camera, you could preen in real time. (Though none of the pictures in this book were taken with one. Pigozzi now uses a Sony RX100.)

These photographs, like the ones in Brassaï's *Graffiti*, foretell a global phenomenon decades in advance. And it's hard to overstate just how global: more than 100 million selfies are now taken every day. "We live in the age of the selfie," the art critic Jerry Saltz wrote in 2014.

But just as Brassaï's pictures of crude Parisian wall markings bear only the faintest resemblance to the elaborate, spray-painted street art of today, so Pigozzi's early selfies, most of which have never been published before, are unmistakably different from the stage-managed, Kardashian-inspired perfection currently darkening the feeds of Instagram. "I'm not interested in glamour, the flowing hair," Pigozzi told *New York*. "I want to show the little second that I find funny in their lives."

"When I started, it was kind of odd and different," Pigozzi says, "but now it's part of the regular world. You do one with your doorman, you do one with your girlfriend, you do one with anything. Taking a selfie is now like shaking somebody's hand."

"[Pigozzi] grabs our 'cosmopolitan' Tel Avivians, stands them in front of what seems like a hundred famous faces—then (*snap*) . . . They think they were being singled out. 'Orna, why is he taking our picture?'" Robert Rosenberg wrote in the *Jerusalem Post Magazine*. "They ask 'Who is this guy' until they turn around and look at the famous faces."

"Yet many of these famous, these visages . . . here, in Israel . . . they are question marks . . . " he wrote. "Can anybody here understand Pigozzi?" ("I'm not so sure we sold anything there," Pigozzi says.)

Pigozzi took a selfie with Rosenberg, an experience that Rosenberg recounted in detail for his readers: "He takes my picture. (*Snap*) outside in the dark where the flash will give the right contrast. He leans and we're cheek to cheek. My arm is at first at my side (*snap*), but for the next (*snap*) yes, he is a new friend, and my arm goes over his shoulder (*snap*), we're new friends, for 15 seconds, Best Friends."

•

"There were a few technical things," Pigozzi says. "First, you had to have a long arm, which I have. Second, you had to use a camera with a slight wide angle lens on it. And number three, you had to use a flash. Not that many people in those days had those three things. Most people with a Leica were purists, so they didn't use a flash. A lot of people who used a flash were reporters. And a lot of people didn't have a long arm like me. There were a lot of elements. And you had to vaguely know what you were doing, because you had to be very fast."

Whatever the reason, Pigozzi was not widely imitated. His pictures did not start a craze, or even a fad. Those who knew him considered Pigozzi's selfie-taking a personal eccentricity of a piece with his love of Memphis design or his habit of pairing Savile Row suits with shirts from Jimmy Jazz. From the seventies through the early years of the twenty-first century, he had the form more or less to himself.

Miller had noticed that interior decorators were warming to photography as a design element, and he decided to nudge the trend along by organizing a group show. “I didn't know anything about anyone,” he says, “but I reached out to a bunch of designers and one thing led to another.” Five firms participated: D'Urso, Falkener-Stuetley, Parish-Hadley, Patino/Wolf, and Mac II. Each was given space within the gallery to create a room centered around one or more photographs. “Now we take that for granted,” Traub says. “There are photographs in every hotel room, every design magazine, blah, blah, blah. But that wasn't always the case.” “I'm told it was very groundbreaking,” Miller says. “I guess it was.”

Patino/Wolf put a custom stainless steel dining table beneath Arnold Newman's portrait of Stravinsky. D'Urso's “listening room” contained a slatted chaise lounge and a small Harry Callahan print of rustling reeds. The reception area and sitting room by Falkener-Stuetley and Parish-Hadley, respectively, were similarly understated. Mica Ertegun and Chessy Rayner, the principals of MAC II, meanwhile, plastered a giant grid of Pigozzi's celebrity selfies across an entire wall. “Now that's done a great deal because you can print it out on big digital printers,” Traub says, “but that was a very unique presentation, particularly for a fine art gallery which was used to putting everything in mattes and metal sections.” According to Miller, “Nobody had done anything like that, anywhere.”

“Pictures in Rooms: Interiors Designed for Photographs,” which doubled as a book party for *Journal of the Seventies*, opened on May 5, 1979. Pigozzi spent the evening snapping pictures of amused partygoers like Jerry Hall, David Johansen, and Anthony Haden-Guest, who covered the event for *New York*, in front of the wall. He took one of himself, too: the first meta-selfie.

Josef Kiriaty, proprietor of the newly opened White Gallery in Tel Aviv's Habima Square, was in New York looking for young photographers to show. Somehow —nobody remembers the exact circumstances—he found Pigozzi. And that October, Pigozzi's selfies were mounted a second time, in Israel.

yet the pictures had a great deal of a kind of social presence. They really got at the idea of collecting all of your friends."

For most of us, taking a picture is a matter of pushing a button. For a photographer, this simple act is made exponentially complicated by the many technical options that must be considered before and after the shutter is released, each turn of the dial marking a shift of allegiance in a long-running aesthetic and epistemological dispute. Where, if anywhere, do Pigozzi's selfies fit into this?

"I think Cartier-Bresson would hate my new book," Pigozzi told *New York*. "He said a photographer must be a hidden observer. I put myself in my pictures. That's how little I am hidden." To do so may have been "astonishingly arrogant" (Wenner), but it was also a frank acknowledgement of artifice—a very Postmodern gesture. And yet because Pigozzi, whether out of principle or laziness, did not retouch or manipulate them any further, his photographs possess a curious integrity. The events might be pseudo, but the images are verité. How to categorize these images? Low Modernism? Documentary Postmodernism? Half-assed Pictorialism?

"Please do not put me between Avedon and Weegee," Pigozzi wrote in the introduction to *Journal of the Seventies*. "I suggest you shelve me between a nice Italian cookbook and The Yellow Pages."

•

The collectible photograph had become "a hot item," *Newsweek* reported in 1974. Diane Arbus prints were going for $1,000 apiece. "There was a point where everybody had to have their turquoise," Larry Miller, Light's then associate director, who now runs the Laurence Miller Gallery on 57th Street, says. "You know, they went to Santa Fe or felt something in their hearts about Native Americans. Well, we became the new turquoise. I really thought it would come and go, but it never went away."

shop; and the Light Gallery, founded in 1971 by Tennyson Schad, which had white walls and displayed photographs in black Nielsen sectional frames. “We wanted to look more like an art gallery, so there were no bins,” Peter MacGill, Light’s first student intern, who went on to cofound Pace/MacGill, says. “We wanted to treat the photographer more like the way painters were treated in other galleries.” “It was a real hothouse for people who just wanted to think about cool, great photographs all the time,” Victor Schrager, the gallery’s director and a friend of Pigozzi’s from Harvard, says.

“We thought we were the first, but as I get farther away, I think it might have been the last of something,” Schrager says. “A lot of other people started approaching the subject from different directions, like Gilbert and George or John Baldessari—people outside the canon of art photography like Robert Cumming, Bill Beckley, Metro Pictures showing Cindy Sherman and Richard Prince, Castelli Graphics . . . Art photography stopped being such a sacrosanct idea for all kinds of different reasons. The great modernist track got kind of dispersed.” (Schrager left Light in 1978 to pursue his own photography.)

“Johnny came in and he had a very different approach to photography’s use,” MacGill says. “Aaron Siskind was trying to transform highly detailed pictures of walls into abstract works of art; Johnny was taking pictures of himself with different women in hotel rooms! He took pictures of things that other people weren’t trying to take pictures of. It was a tremendous breath of visual fresh air when he would bring them in. It was fun!” “It was also about conquest,” Charles Traub, who succeeded Schrager as gallery director and is now chair of the MFA Photo/Video program at the School of Visual Arts in New York, says. “It was about the fact that everyone was a participant, everyone was on display and wanted to be on display.”

“He used these little point-and-shoot cameras,” Traub says, “not big fancy cameras that the usual fine art people who we represented would use. And seventies "turns around the new jet-setting, where room service is a fact of daily life, and where it is important to be rich, any way you can get there."

"There is a case," Wenner wrote, "for the snapshot's aptness to the current historical moment. We live in a time of regal celebrity. Fame, no matter what kind, is nothing to be ashamed about; to be talked about is to be alive. With the mounting importance of who is where, and particularly with whom, it naturally follows that the paparazzi has become the master of modern portraiture." (Yet Pigozzi was no paparazzo. Though his photographs are formally similar, in their indifference to form, to the kind taken by professionals like Ron Galella or amateurs like Gary Lee Boas, there is one very important difference: they were on the outside looking in; "I get in," Pigozzi told *New York*.)

The pictures are organized by subject: parties, hotel rooms, food ("Indigestion"), dogs, and so on. There is a page titled "New Sounds," listing disco, *Deep Throat*, "The 18-minute gap," and Susan Sontag, among other seventies phenomena. And then there is "Pigozzi & Co.": forty-five pictures of various celebrities—an exuberant Iman, a deadpan John Belushi, Hunter S. Thompson with his trademark cigarette holder, Candice Bergen with a pair of oversize sunglasses, and Pelé without a shirt, to name a few—with Pigozzi, by Pigozzi. "The current total of these self-portraits," Wenner wrote, "is at least twenty times more than what's shown here." To Wenner, these "astonishingly arrogant and thoroughly amusing" pictures represented "the ultimate fantasy of the fan in everyone: A picture of yourself with your favorite star. Conquests! Self-immortalization!"

"When seen as a whole," he added, "another meaning to this series becomes quite clear: myself, above all others, as the star."

•

In 1978, there were two galleries in New York devoted to photography: Witkin, founded in 1969 by Lee Witkin, which resembled an old print

Most of his subjects were sporting, like Ms. Dunaway. But not all: Patti Smith "went crazy," Pigozzi told *New York* magazine. "She said, 'No, you can't do that!' So I didn't even try. I walked away."

"In the seventies," he says now, "people had no idea what I was doing."

•

Ratazzi introduced Pigozzi to Jean-Claude Suares, the design director of *New York*, who sent him on a few local assignments for the magazine. Pigozzi was interested in publishing a book of his personal photographs, "but I had no idea how to do that," he says, so he asked Suares's advice. Suares took a look at the pictures, liked what he saw, and introduced Pigozzi to Lindy Hess, an editor at Doubleday, where she was mentoring Jackie Onassis. "[Hess] said, 'Okay, let's do the book,'" Pigozzi says. Jane Wenner, Michele Napear, an artist, Christine Zea, a production designer, and Paul Josefowitz, a friend from Harvard, helped edit the pictures, and Suares designed the layout.

"Some people are in this book because they are very important for the '70s," Pigozzi wrote in the preface of *Pigozzi's Journal of the Seventies*. "Some are here because I love them. And some are here because my classy editor at Doubleday, Lindy Hess, felt it would make the book more commercial." In the acknowledgements, he thanks his professor Bob Fulton and "all the wonderful people at Harvard for giving me a diploma," Leica "for building my camera," "La Famiglia Ratazzi for their generous hospitality and wonderful home-made lasagna," and finally, "My Mother, for not sending me to a factory when I was 12, Central Color for not scratching too many negatives, and The May '68 Revolution for not having changed anything."

"I believe that the seventies didn't begin until 1977," Jann Wenner wrote in the book's introduction, dated November 1978. "The *real* seventies was a period in which the post-sixties search for meaning was found to be pointless and premature. It was a time of rejection of meaning." The world of the actress Léa Seydoux). “Gaumont was thinking of merging or doing something with Fox, so they sent me for five or six months to Los Angeles,” Pigozzi says. “They sent me for two reasons: One, I could speak English. Nobody at Gaumont really spoke English. And number two, they didn’t really pay me, so it was not expensive for them.”

One day on the Fox lot, he met Mel Brooks, who took him out for lunch at Canter’s delicatessen. Another day, by the pool of the Beverly Hills Hotel, Delfina Ratazzi introduced him to Ahmet Ertegun. “Ahmet and I were wearing exactly the same Smedley polo shirt,” Pigozzi says. “It was like a deluxe Lacoste—a very English thing. He was very impressed that this young man would have one. We became instant friends over that.”

Pigozzi returned to Paris, but spent three or four months each year in New York, staying either with Jann and Jane Wenner, the founders of *Rolling Stone*, whom he had met through Max Palevsky, an early tech investor, or at the Carlyle Hotel. Between Ratazzi, the Erteguns, the Wenners, and the Jaggers—he’d met Bianca through a mutual friend named François Wimille, the son of a Grand Prix champion, in Paris—Pigozzi was now one degree from all the decade’s big players, and he recorded each noteworthy encounter by taking a selfie. (In 1991, he took one with my father, Graydon Carter, and Kurt Andersen, then the editors of *Spy* magazine, which Pigozzi briefly owned.)

“I was always amazed that people would ask for autographs from movie stars or from sports people,” Pigozzi says. “How does it really prove that you met the person? If you have a selfie, it shows that you’re standing next to the Pope or Taylor Swift or Mick Jagger.”

“I would only take one. I’d look straight into the lens and keep the camera at eye level. And I would use a flash,” he says. “Some didn’t turn out. I remember one of Julie Christie looking ugly. There was no way to know if you took it right, of course. And you only got one shot. Back then, it took about ten seconds to wind the camera and take a picture.”

"I think the only conventional thing Johnny did at Harvard was he joined one of the eating clubs," Sagansky says. "Now so many of the students are foreign, but then it was rather unusual. It was still a Northeastern school. Johnny completely stood out. Everybody knew him, or knew of him. And yet he wasn't somebody who participated in a lot of extracurricular activities—at least not organized Harvard extracurricular activities. He would disappear on weekends and go down to New York and come back with these incredible stories and these incredible pictures." On such weekends, Pigozzi flew Eastern Airlines ("It cost seventeen dollars for students, and you could pay on the plane") and stayed with his friend Delfina Ratazzi, a well-connected member of the Agnelli family who had an apartment on the Upper East Side.

Robert Fulton III, a visual studies professor and experimental filmmaker distantly related to the famous steamboat builder, introduced Pigozzi to Robert Frank's *The Americans*. "[Frank] took pictures of people in diners, or sitting in their car, or waiting around offices, and that's what I found so fantastic," Pigozzi says. "His pictures are about the normal, not any kind of drama or basketball players jumping. He got the Guggenheim [Fellowship] and traveled across America. I was stuck at Harvard, so I took pictures of what was around. I'm a very lazy photographer."

"The other students would go and take beautiful pictures of trees in Maine," Pigozzi says. "I took pictures of dogs with a flash in their face. Nobody was doing that. I did an entire series on cars that were damaged in accidents. In Cambridge, because of the snow, a lot of cars would crash into each other. I never tried to do pretty pictures."

In June 1974, Pigozzi graduated and moved back to Paris. An uncle, Enrico Beretta, who owned a company called Technifil that manufactured shopping carts, gave him a job. "I was an okay salesman," he says. "Not incredible, not bad. But I didn't think this was the future for me." Then a Harvard classmate named Emmanuel Schlumberger introduced Pigozzi to his cousin, Nicolas Seydoux, chairman of the French film studio Gaumont (and uncle of the very difficult to use Leica when I was about ten or eleven. I took pictures of dogs or people around me. I was always very interested in having a journal of my life, but I can't read my own handwriting. I would write things down, and then . . . *you know* . . . This way, I could record everything I did and I saw." Pigozzi started carrying a camera around "360 days a year."

"I was dyslexic, so I didn't do very well in school," he says. "In those days, they didn't know what dyslexia was—they just thought you were stupid. It was not a happy childhood. I wanted to learn new things, see new things, experiment with new things. The French culture was turned to the past."

When the time came, Pigozzi applied to the only two American universities he had heard of: Harvard and Yale. He didn't get into Yale. "And I didn't get into Harvard because my SATs were so brilliant," he says. "You had to have an interview with an old alumni, and I was interviewed by a very nice man in Paris who worked for a bank called the Irving Trust. He asked me, 'Where are you from originally?' And I said, my parents are from Torino. He said, 'Ah! I know Torino very well.' Then he said, 'I'm going to ask you two questions. If you get them right, I'll get you into Harvard.' I said okay. He said, 'What's the best restaurant in Torino?' I said, 'Gatto Nero, the black cat.' Next question: 'What's the season for white truffles?' I said, 'October to November.' He said, 'Okay, I'll get you into Harvard.'"

Pigozzi enrolled as a freshman in the fall of 1970. "It was the end of the '60s," Jeff Sagansky, a classmate and friend who became an entertainment executive, says. "There was one riot in Harvard Square our freshman year, and then things quieted down, classes graduated on time. There were protests because we were still in Vietnam, but they didn't disrupt the university. Things were changing, you could see it. By the time we graduated, the war was over and the whole mindset of the country had changed. There were people going to business school and law school. All those guys who eventually became the hedge fund managers and the private equity funds—it was just the beginning of that."

CHEEK TO CHEEK

ASH CARTER

In February 1974, Faye Dunaway was named "Woman of the Year" by Harvard's Hasty Pudding Club. According to *Newsweek*, "she was honored with a motorcade, a brass pudding pot and the stimulation of a question-and-answer session with Harvard types. Q: Why didn't you shave your armpits in a *Vogue* layout? Faye: 'I didn't want to.' Waddaya think of Bebe Rebozo? 'I don't have any opinion on Bebe Rebozo.'"

After the ceremony, a twenty-two-year-old senior named Jean Christophe Pigozzi—the same student who, though not a club member, had asked the honoree about her underarm hair—sidled up to Dunaway, held out his Leica M4, aimed its wide-angle lens somewhere between the two of them, and took what we would now call a selfie.

And, over the next four decades, he took hundreds more with other famous actors and actresses, artists and art dealers, filmmakers, fashion designers, writers, rock stars, superagents, athletes, royals, models, moguls, publicists, journalists, comedians, scenesters, gadflies, and miscellaneous personalities who defined international celebrity and social life in the late twentieth and early twenty-first centuries—as well as his barber, a Turkish belly dancer, a busload of Japanese tourists, Andy Warhol's stuffed dog, an Oscar, and a BLT.

"There were people taking self-portraits for a hundred years. They would put the camera on a tripod with a long tube and a little pump and you'd press it and take your picture," Pigozzi says. "But people doing it the way I did it? I never saw anybody doing that." That doesn't mean it didn't happen, of course. But Pigozzi's body of work in the genre, brought together here for the first time, is unequaled. Verily, he is the rightful selfie king.

•

"I started taking pictures very early," Pigozzi, who grew up in Paris, says. "My father [Henri, who started the French car company Simca] gave me this old,

ME, 1979

ME + FAYE DUNAWAY, 2016

ME + NOBUYOSHI ARAKI, 2017

CATE BLANCHETT + ME, 2008

ROBERT DE NIRO + ME, 2009

ME + ED RUSCHA, 2012

DAPHNE GUINNESS + ME, 2008

ME + WOODY ALLEN, 2016

ME + MARTHA STEWART + DOG, 2016

ME + BRETT RATNER, 2007

ME + MAURIZIO CATTELAN SCULPTURE OF STEPHANIE SEYMOUR, 2010

PHARRELL WILLIAMS + ME, 2009

PRINCESS OLGA OF GREECE + ME, 2007

ME + LADY GAGA, 2012

ME + NICOLAS BERGGRUEN, 2008

ME + UMA THURMAN, 2015

DANIEL CRAIG + ME, 2008

ME + FOREST WHITAKER, 2008

ME + CATHERINE ZETA JONES, 2008

ME + CATHERINE DENEUVE, 2017

ME + LAPO ELKANN + COCO BRANDOLINI, 2007

ME + RAT, 2008

XIANG JING'S *YOUR BODY* + ME, 2008

ME + ANNA HABER, 2011

JOHN BALDESSARI + ME, 2006

ME + JEFFREY DEITCH, 2013

BRUCE WEBER + ME, 2010

PARIS HILTON + ME, 2009

ME + BOB COLACELLO, 2009

URSULA ANDRESS + ME, 2008

ME + HAT SALESMAN IN ST. TROPEZ, 2014

WOMAN IN A BLACK LACE DRESS + ME, 2011

ME + KIRK DOUGLAS, 2015

ME + XIN LI + PETER BEARD, 2011

SHARON STONE + ME, 2006

ME + MARIO TESTINO, 2015

CALVIN KLEIN + ME, 2015

JOEL SILVER + ME, 2014

MIKE TYSON + ME, 2009

ME + CHER, 2016

XIN LI + ME, 2009

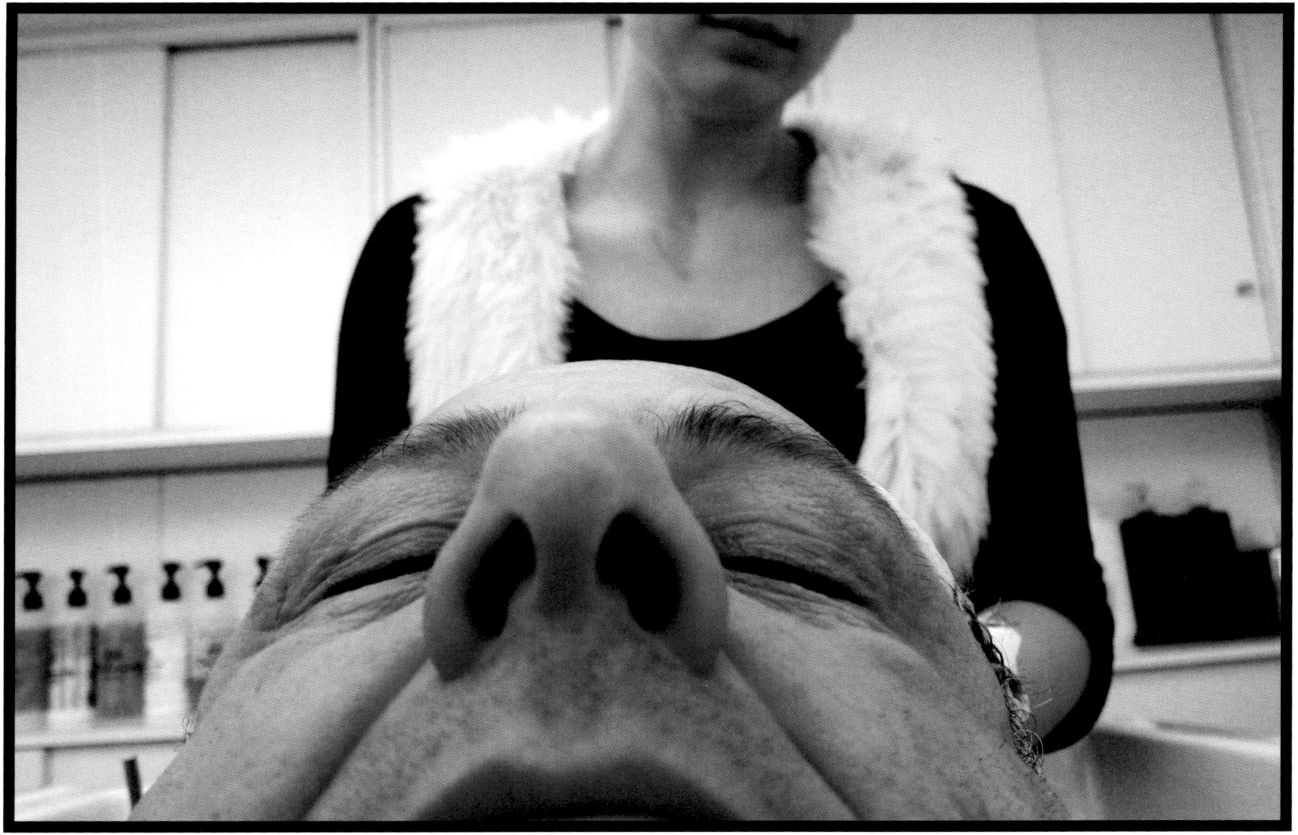

ME + SHAMPOO TECHNICIAN, 2011

MAO ZEDONG + ME, 2013

ME + SARAH JESSICA PARKER, 2016

ME + SALMAN RUSHDIE, 2007

NILE RODGERS + ME, 2013

ME + MARC JACOBS, 2008

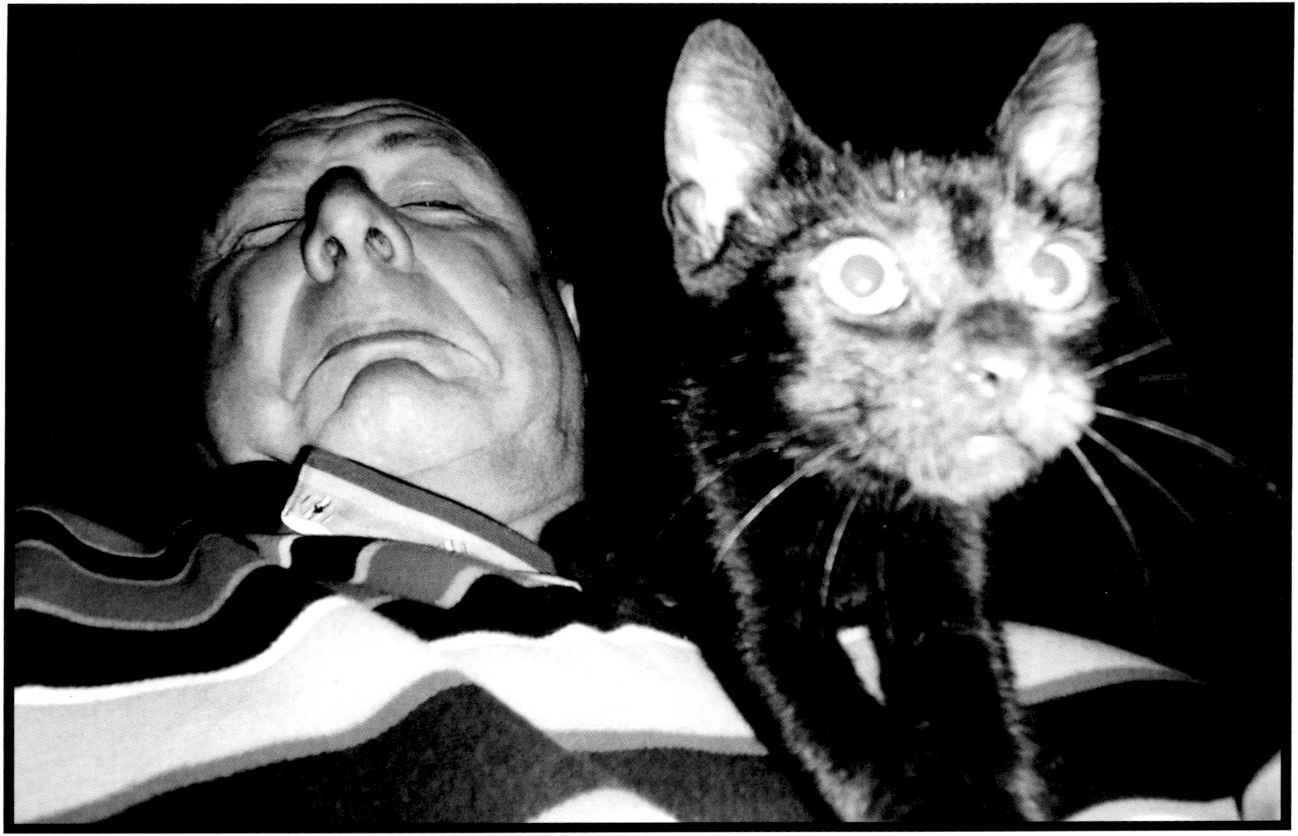

ME + CAT, 2008

ME + ERINA MATSUI, 2011

ME + TAKASHI MURAKAMI, 2015

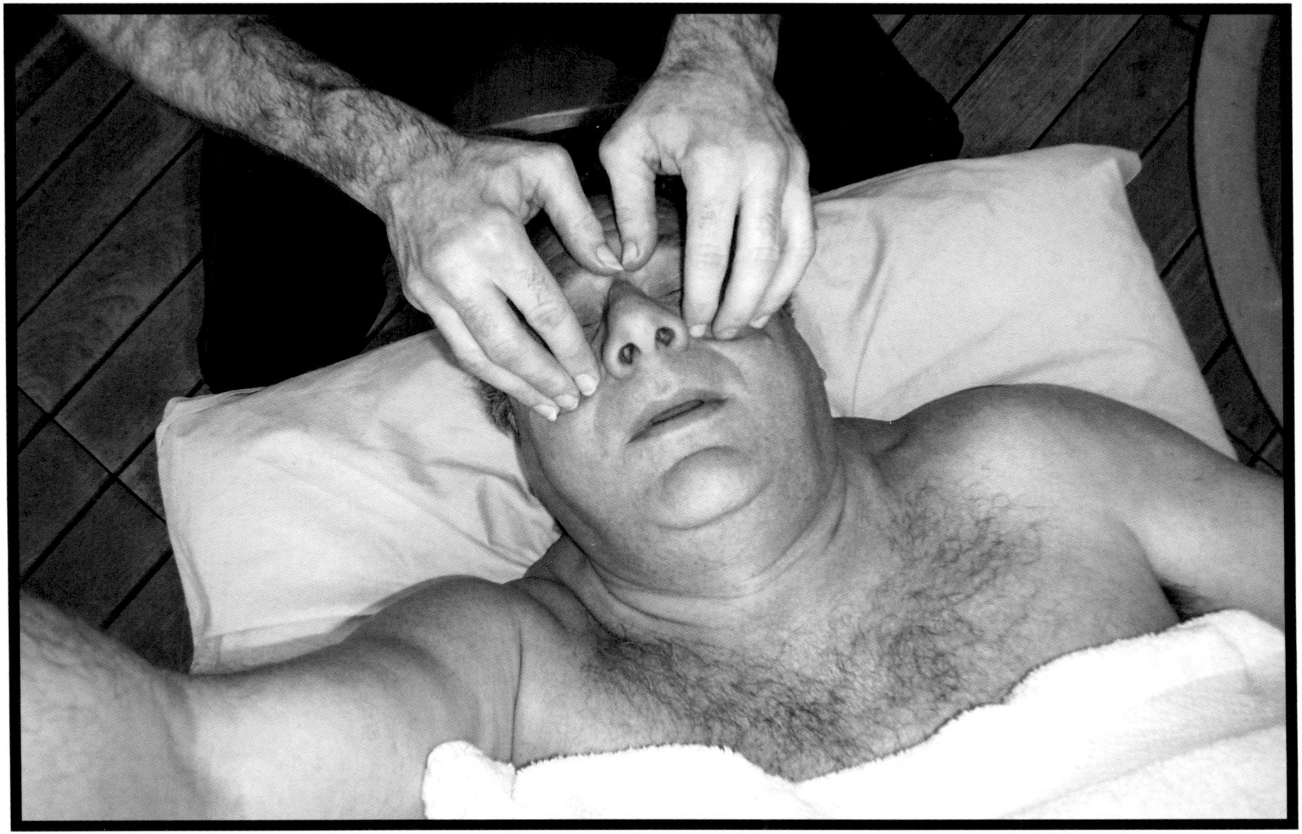

ME + MASSEUR, 2008

ME + AI WEIWEI + MAURIZIO CATTELAN, 2016

CINDY SHERMAN + ME, 2008

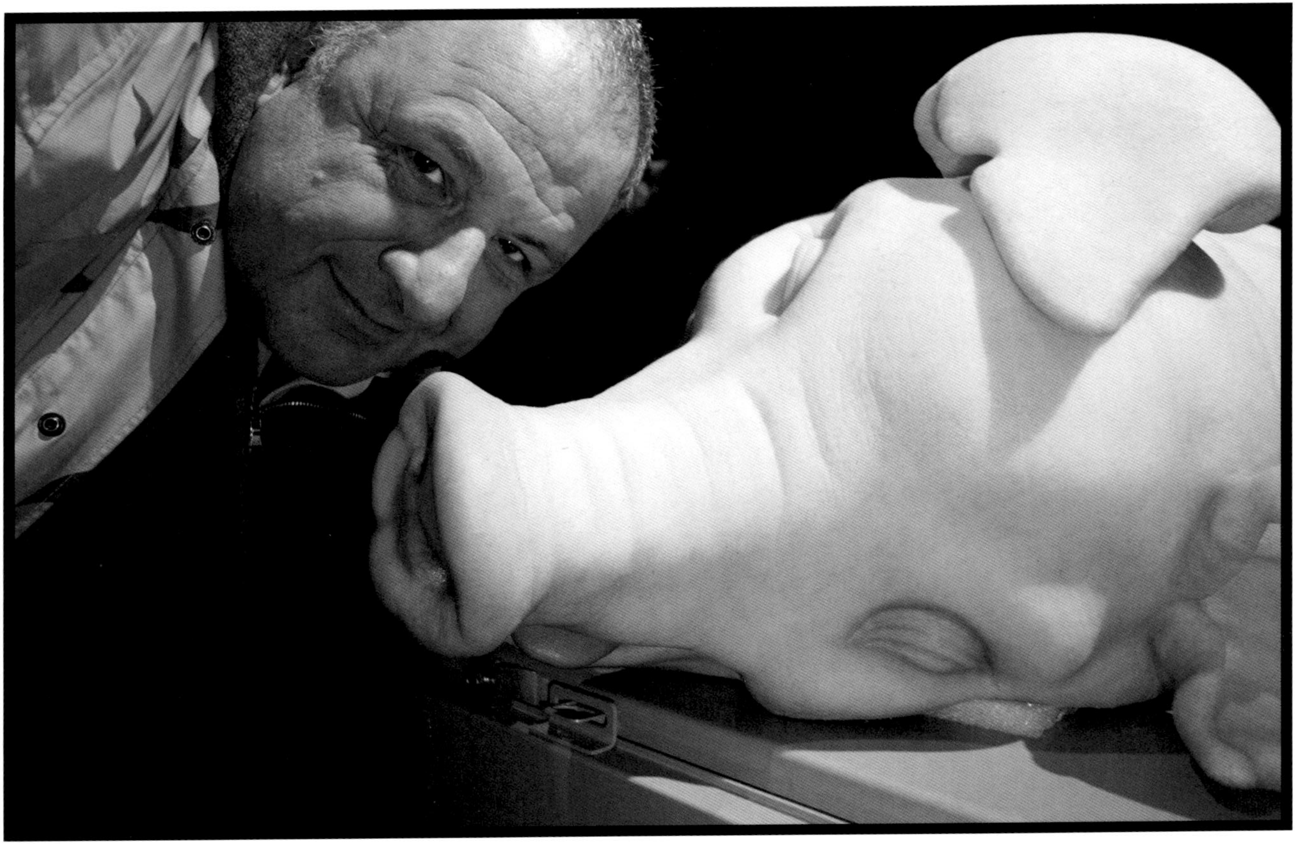

ME + PAUL MCCARTHY'S *MECHANICAL PIG*, 2014

ME + COURTNEY LOVE, 2010

OSCAR + ME, 2009

ME + MICK JAGGER + SEAN PENN, 2009

ME + BRUCE HOEKSEMA + BARRY DILLER, 2011

ME + MONICA LEWINSKY, 2016

ME + MICHAEL DOUGLAS, 2009

GEISHA + ME, 2008

HELENA CHRISTENSEN + BONO + ME, 2010

WIM WENDERS + ME, 2007

ME + CROCODILE, 2015

ME + JUNE NEWTON, 2008

ME + CARRIE FISHER, 2016

USHER + ME, 2010

ME + LARRY GAGOSIAN, 2015

ME + GRACE JONES, 2011

ME + CHARLIE ROSE, 2009

ME + BETTE MIDLER + PRINCESS FIRYAL OF JORDAN, 2007

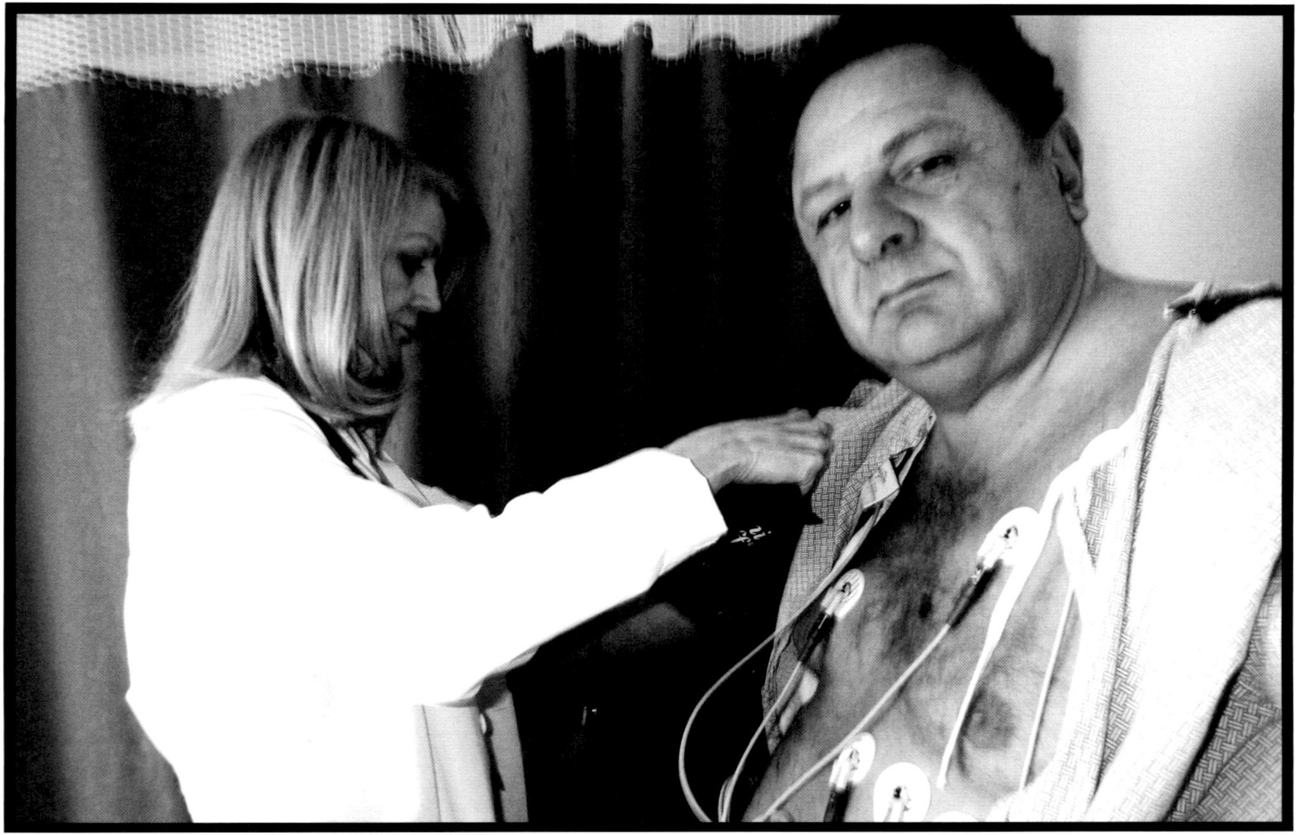

DOCTOR + ME, 2007

KRISTEN MCMENAMY + ME, 2016

ME + A PORTRAIT OF DAKIS JOANNOU BY ROBERTO CUOGHI, 2008

KITTY AFTER FALLING OFF HER BICYCLE + ME, 1990

DAN RATHER + ME, 1980

FRANCESCA THYSSEN + ME, 1984

INÈS DE LA FRESSANGE + ME, 1985

KURT ANDERSEN + GRAYDON CARTER + ME, 1991

CLINT EASTWOOD + ME, 1985

FRAN LEBOWITZ + ME, 1979

BELLY DANCER IN BODRUM, TURKEY + ME, 1989

JERRY ZIPKIN + ME, 1986

CHINESE SOLDIER + ME, 1980

ME + MALCOLM MCLAREN, 1992

PAUL JOSEFOWITZ + JEFF SAGANSKY + ME, 1985

KING SUNNY ADÉ + ME, 1983

DAVID KELLEY + ME, 1984

EL_E MACPHERSON + ME, 1988

HERBIE HANCOCK + ME, 1985

MATHILDA MAY + ME, 1987

FRANCIS FORD COPPOLA + ME, 1986

DAME EDNA EVERAGE + ME, 1992

SYLVESTER STALLONE + ME, 1993

MICK FLEETWOOD + ME, 1982

ANDY WARHOL + ME, 1986

VIOLIN + ME, 1988

MEL BROOKS + ME, 1988

ROMUALD HAZOUMÈ + ME, 1992

JERRY MOSS + ME, 1986

VALERIE PERRINE + ME, 1979

NORMAN MAILER + ME, 1977

JOHN PHILLIPS + ME, 1976

ME + PICASSO'S *LES DEMOISELLES D'AVIGNON*, 1978

JONI MITCHELL + ME, 1978

NEIL SIMON + ME, 1977

LOULOU DE LA FALAISE + ME, 1978

RON GALELLA + ME, 1978

SERGIO LEONE + ME, 1978

IMAN + ME, 1977

CHRISTOPHER REEVE + ME, 1979

B.B. KING + ME, 1979

TENNYSON SCHAD + ME, 1979

GILDA RADNER + ME, 1978

ME + ARNOLD SCHWARZENEGGER, 1977

HUNTER S. THOMPSON + ME, 1977

CHERYL LADD + ME, 1979

SWIFTY LAZAR + ME + JERRY ZIPKIN, 1979

THE EMPIRE STATE BUILDING + ME, 1978

MIKE NICHOLS + ME, 1978

ART GARFUNKEL + ME, 1975

DAVID HOCKNEY + ME, 1977

JASMINE + ME, 1977

ROD STEWART + ME, 1978

PAUL MORRISSEY + ME, 1979

MARTIN SCORSESE + ME, 1978

CANDICE BERGEN + ME, 1977

ERIC IDLE + ME, 1978

SWIFTY LAZAR + ME, 1978

PATTY OJA + ME, 1978

JOHN BELUSHI + ME, 1977

EVA IONESCO + ME, 1978

BEAR + ME, 1979

JERRY HALL + ME + MICK JAGGER, 1978

ME + JAPANESE TOURISTS IN FLORENCE, 1978

WARHOL'S STUFFED DOG AT THE FACTORY + ME, 1978

GIAN CARLO BUSSEI + ME, 1978

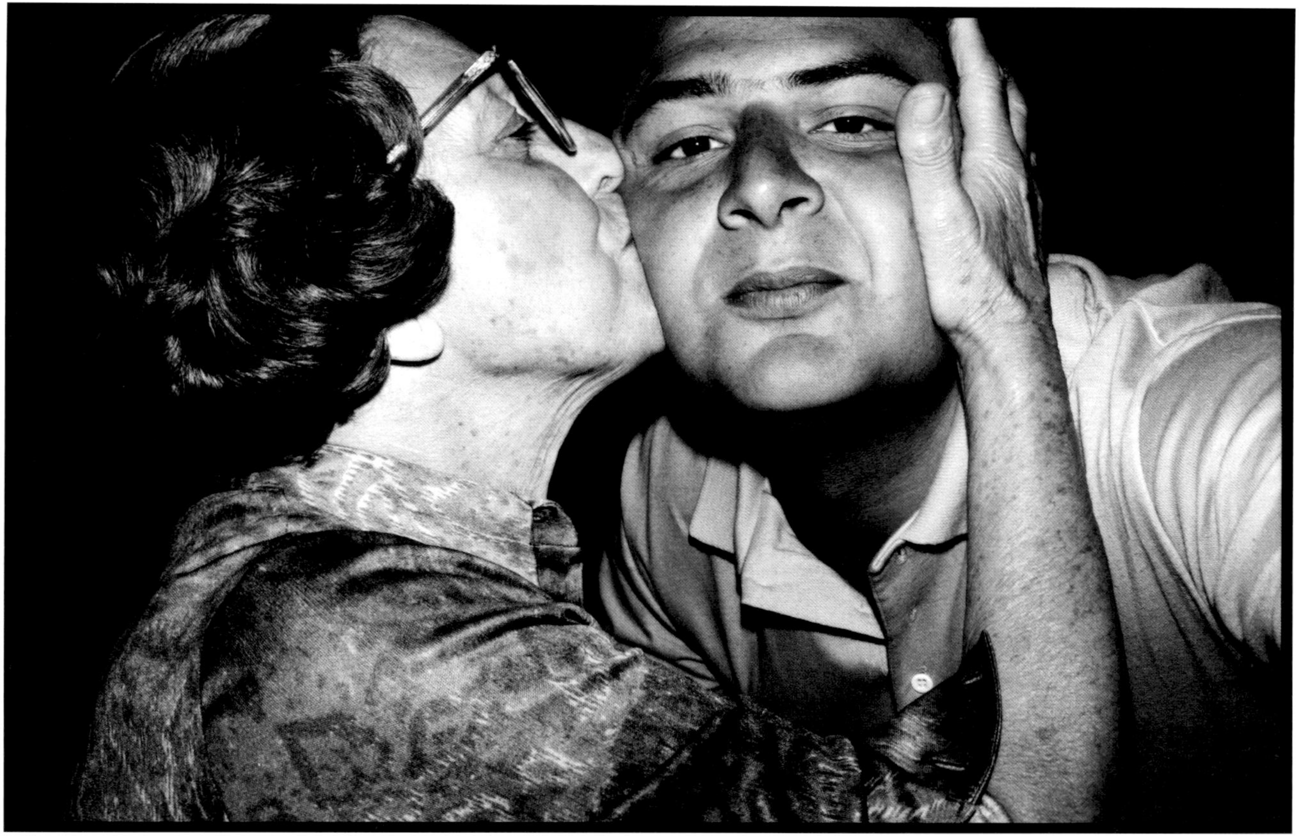

LA MIA MAMMA + ME, 1977

STEVE MARTIN + ME, 1977

ME + A FRIEND, 1977

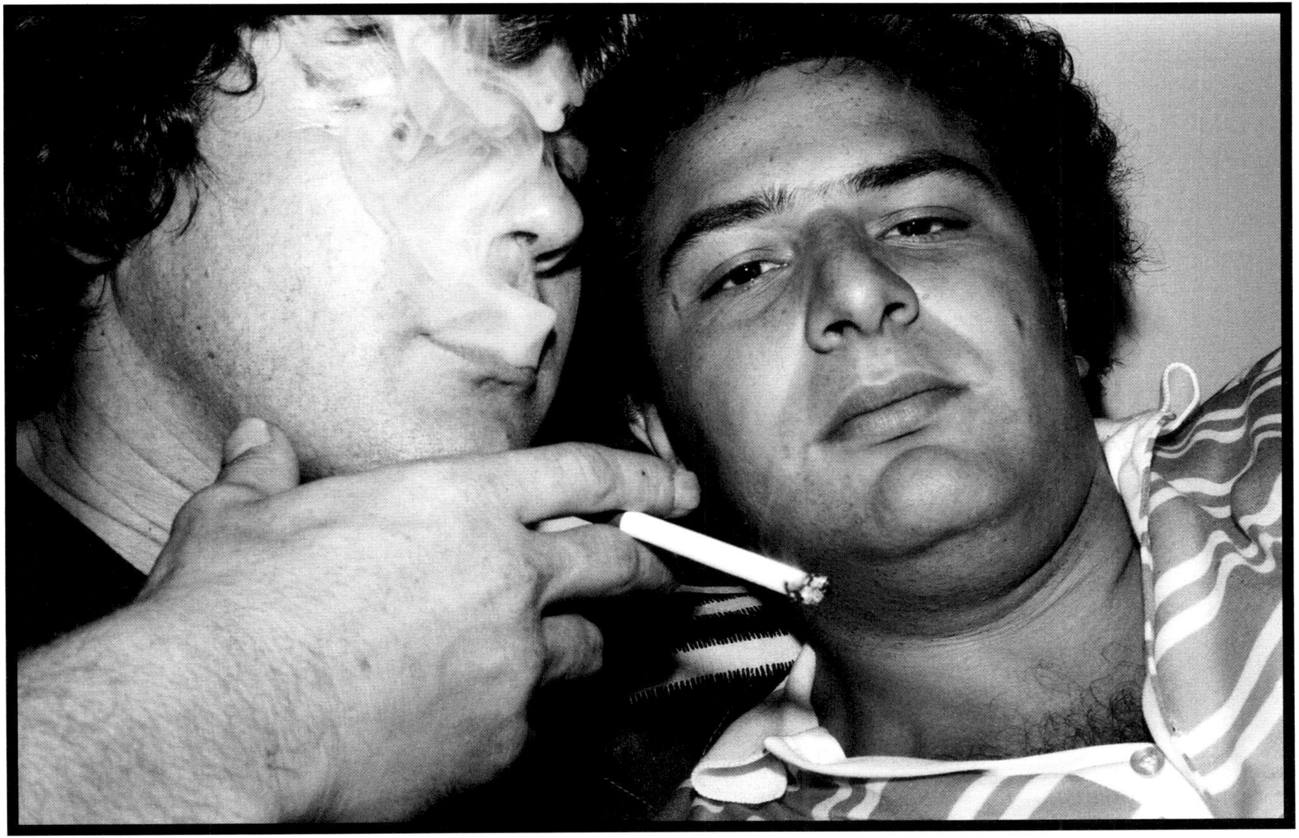

JANN WENNER + ME, 1977

TIMOTHY LEARY + ME, 1978

HEAD VALET AT THE BEVERLY HILLS HOTEL, CHRIS DUNN + ME, 1977

MARISA BERENSON + ME, 1978

ME + RINGO STARR, 1978

PELÉ + ME, 1977

JULIE CHRISTIE + ME, 1977

MARIO PUZO + ME, 1978

MACKENZIE PHILLIPS + ME + A FRIEND, 1975

DOLLY PARTON + ME, 1977

I invented the selfie (but not the word *selfie*).

I use a Leica with a flash.

I have long arms.

I am dyslexic.

Selfies are much better than autographs as they
really prove that you met the person in the photo next to you.

— Jean Pigozzi, Geneva, May 2017

FAYE DUNAWAY + ME, 1973